The Kintsugi Kid

Allison Mathis Jones

Editor: Pen2Paper Editorial, LLC

Dedication

To Harper: Thank you for showing me that
even in all of my imperfection, I'm still the perfect mama
for you. Thank you for reminding me that my broken is
beautiful in the most mundane ways—with the hugs you
didn't know I needed, the sweet kisses that made my
heart skip a beat, and the reassuring smiles that gave me
the confidence that I needed to press on, even on the
messiest days.

Little curly Pearl was a whirly, whirly girl. And like most whirly girls curly Pearl loved to twirl.

At the park, in the store, and even at home, Pearl just couldn't help it—twirling was her favorite way to roam.

One day, Pearl twirled past a colorful book adorned with a shimmery bowl.

The bowl on the cover was special because its cracks were filled with gold.

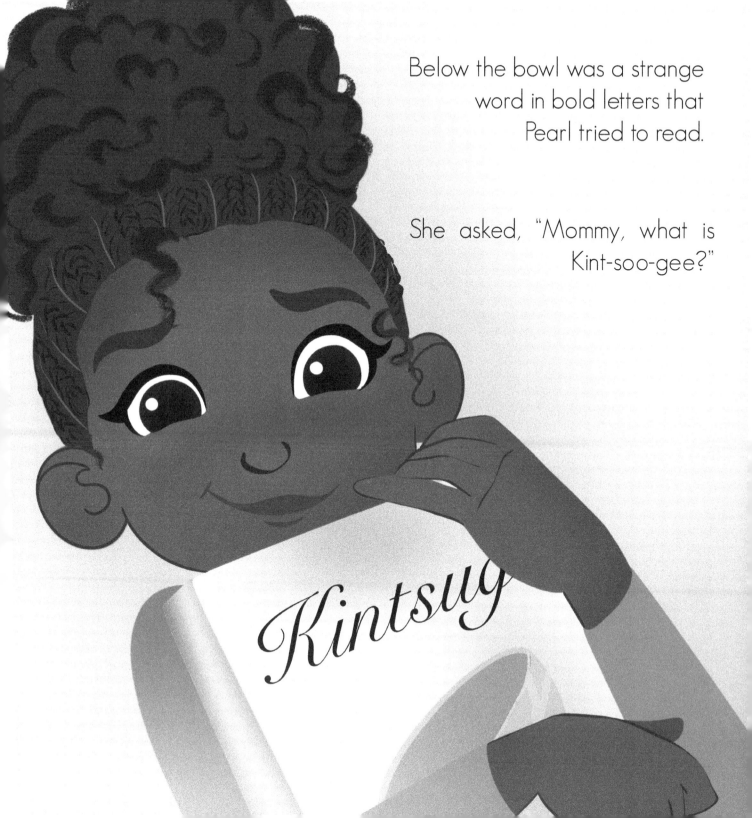

Below the bowl was a strange word in bold letters that Pearl tried to read.

She asked, "Mommy, what is Kint-soo-gee?"

Kintsug

"Kintsugi is a way to make broken things pretty again!"
"Daddy and I learned about it during our time in Japan."

Pearl said, "I can't wait to share this with my friends!" She smiled at Mommy and then continued to spin.

She twirled over here. She twirled over there. Mommy warned her to be careful, but curly Pearl didn't care. In the blink of an eye, Pearl started twirling just a little too fast.

She crashed into the table as she quickly whirled past. The table wobbled wildly and on her face she fell flat. Cups and plates went flying to the floor, with a boom and a splat!

Mommy ran over and scooped Pearl into a hug. "Don't worry sweet Pearl, Doc Brown will stitch you right up!"

Doc Brown sewed Pearl's cut and as he sent Pearl on her way, he told her that her new scar was more than likely there to stay.

Pearl couldn't believe it. She looked down at the ground and said, "Oh, what have I done? I think I've ruined my face, and I was only trying to have fun."

Mommy said, "It's ok, baby. That scar gives you flair!"

"But Mommy, having a scar like this just doesn't seem fair."

Pearl sulked all the way home, but when she arrived, she was greeted by Daddy who had a special surprise.

"When something falls and breaks, we don't just throw it away."
"You see this plate? It's not trash—it still can be great!"

"We'll take all the broken pieces and make something better. This plate will be perfect when we put it back together." Daddy and Pearl used glue that shimmered and shined. The plate was like a puzzle—all the pieces aligned.

As Pearl stood back and proudly admired their work, she was instantly reminded of her own little quirk. Pearl remembered that kintsugi is about making broken things whole. Kintsugi makes things more beautiful because they are mended with gold.

"Daddy, I don't think kintsugi only works on glass. We are all like kintsugi, we all get a chance! Sometimes things happen that just don't seem fair, but as Mommy said, my new scar gives me my own special flair!"

"That's right!" Daddy said. "Like this plate that we've made more beautiful than before, your scar will be a symbol of strength forevermore."

So your blemish, your chipped tooth, your big squiggly scar—yes, it will be with you wherever you are. But don't be afraid. There's no need to worry. Think of it as a chance to share your story. Own your imperfections because they make you, you! Always remember, your broken is beautiful too.

About The Author

Meet
Allison Mathis Jones

Allison is the author of *The Kintsugi Kid* and is also a "kintsugi kid" herself. Health and wellness are important to the University of Miami graduate who has a background in mental health and a master's degree in marriage and family therapy. After recovering from a brain tumor removal, Allison became intrigued by the parallel of the Japanese art-form kintsugi and its process of repairing broken objects with gold lacquer. She felt that this art-form related to her own unintentional brokenness and healing experience. Allison holds the belief that all people have little gold-filled cracks with shimmering traces that tell unique stories of resilience and renewal. Allison launched Kintsugi Candle Co.® and has become a beacon of hope to many as she encourages others to revel in their brokenness and embark on a journey of healing. Through her company, Allison shares her love of aromatic scented candles to demonstrate the importance of practicing self-care and self-love. Allison is originally from Georgia, but has traded in her Southern belle attire for a multitude of suitcases and passport stamps as she globetrots with her husband and sweet daughter. The Jones trio is currently living in Japan, but carry Georgia in their hearts. When Allison is not spending time with her family or influencing her growing audience on social media, she can be found as a featured guest on tons of family blogs spreading messages of healing, hope, and happiness.

To learn more about Allison and her endeavors, visit:
https://allisonmathisjones.com/
To stay up-to-date with all things Kintsugi Kid, visit
https://thekintsugikid.com/

 @allisonmathisjones

 www.facebook.com/allisonmathisjones